Prayers for Peace of Mind and Heart

by
Joseph P. Laruffa

ST. PAUL BOOKS & MEDIA

BOSTON

Nihil Obstat
   Rev. Richard V. Lawlor, SJ
   Censor Deputatus

Imprimatur
   +Humberto Cardinal Medeiros
   Archbishop of Boston

ISBN 0-8198-5866-8

Printed and published by Pauline Books & Media,
50 St. Paul's Avenue, Boston, MA 02130.

Pauline Books & Media is the publishing house of the
Daughters of St. Paul, an international congregation of women
religious serving the Church with the communications media.

Contents

DAILY PRAYERS

A Prayer for the Emotionally Afflicted

Dear Jesus, I plead for strength and consolation
for myself
and for all who suffer emotionally.

In face of fear, may we have the grace to act as
You did
in the Garden of Gethsemane,
where You became so fearful that You sweated
blood.
Let us be strong, courageous, humble and
resigned
as You were in the Garden that Holy Thursday
night.

Besides fear, we face terrible periods of
depression.
May we have the grace to wait patiently and
calmly
until our fearful and darkened hours pass away.

May we have the grace not to become fright-
ened
over violent temptations, strange thoughts
and periods of nervous depression and spiritual
gloom.

Help us not to panic at such trying times!
Help us to hold on to You.

Hold our trembling hands with Your pierced
    hands!
And still our terror-filled hearts with the sound
    of Your voice!

May we, dear Jesus,
have the grace to say "yes" to You whenever
    You see fit
to invite us to suffer with You in the Garden of
    Olives.
How can we refuse to suffer for You,
who suffered so much for us, even mentally?

May we have the grace to accept ourselves as
    we are
—with our melancholic temperaments; our
    many limitations, weaknesses,
fears and faults.

May we have the grace to love You dearly;
to trust in You; to believe that You are always
    with us,
no matter how difficult or dark things may be-
    come.

May we have the grace to remember that
    nothing can happen to us,
without Your consent, and the grace to place
    our weak and sick selves
under Your tender protection and fatherly care.

Jesus, may Your grace flood our souls;
Your light flood our minds,
and Your peace flood our hearts!

A Prayer to the Divine Physician

Feet of the divine Physician,
come to me.
Hands of the divine Physician,
rest on me; bless me; cure me.
Arms of the divine Physician,
enfold me in a loving embrace of peace.
Eyes of the divine Physician,
see my misery of soul, mind and body,
and take pity on me.
Ears of the divine Physician,
hear my cries; listen to my complaints.
Lips of the divine Physician,
speak to me; console me.
Body of the divine Physician,
be my sure remedy.
Blood of the divine Physician,
be my refreshment; my cure-all medicine.
Heart of the divine Physician,
love me tenderly.
Soul of the divine Physician,
spiritualize my physical troubles
and mental anguish.
Divinity of Christ,
heal my soul, mind and body.
Amen.

A Prayer to Jesus in Time of Sickness

My divine Savior, Jesus Christ,
Your holy name of Jesus
is a most powerful name,
and I call on it with full confidence
of being heard.
My sweet Jesus,
be the health of my body;
the light of my mind;
the delight of my heart;
the peace of my soul;
the great joy of my life.

Jesus,
in time of weakness,
   be my fortitude;
in periods of doubt,
   be my safeguard;
in desolation,
   be my sole consolation;
in darkness of spirit,
   be my light;
in time of failure,
   be my steady support.

Dear Jesus,
in time of disquiet,
   be my peace;
in moments when tempted to despair,
   be my unfailing hope;
in sickness of body, mind or soul,
   be my healing ointment;
in loneliness,
   be my constant companion,
   my comforter;
in time of weariness,
   be my rest;
in death,
   be my eternal reward.

A Prayer for Mental Health

O Lord,
Too often we feel the blues.
We are lonely, gloomy, full of mental woes.
We are too easily depressed, discouraged, dis-
    heartened.
Our daily efforts appear dry, barren, useless.
We often feel weary of life itself—
And almost driven to the pit of black despair.

And so we come to You,
Dear Jesus,
Divine Physician,
Great healer of souls, minds and bodies,
With a great sense of urgency,
Begging for assistance,
Seeking guidance,
Looking for encouragement,
Strength and consolation.

O Lord,
Uplift us.
Clear our minds of all doubts and confusion;
Free them of all gloomy images;
Let them be fixed on bright,
Cheerful and peaceful thoughts.

O Jesus,
Help us to be full of gladness and optimism.

Instill in us
The virtue of lively hope.
Help us to be humble enough
To be satisfied with our lot in life.
May we have the grace
To accept
All our mental pains and anguishes.
And may we have the grace
To wait patiently
Until our darkened hours pass away,
As indeed they will.

O Lord,
Help us to open our eyes wide—
To enjoy the light;
To see the sun, moon and stars;
The grass, trees and flowers;
The smiles on friendly faces.

Help us to open our ears—
To hear the sounds of the wind and of music;
The sounds of the birds and children at play.

O Jesus,
Help us to open our mouths—
To sing Your praises;
To speak of Your love,
Mercy, goodness and beauty.

Let us extend our hands to You—
To warmly receive from You
All the blessings and joys
You send to us daily.

O Lord,
Help us to open our hearts—
To receive Your love.
Assist us to forget self
And to think of others.
Aid us to love all.

O divine Physician,
Our souls are opened to You:
Fill them
With Your light and grace;
Your joy and peace.

A Litany of the Holy Face of Christ

Face of Christ, the holy face of God,*
Face of Christ, well-pleasing to God, the Father,
Face of Christ, perfect image of Mary, Your blessed Mother,
Face of Christ, delight and joy of the angels,
Face of Christ, adored and loved by all the saints,
Face of Christ, brighter than the sun,
Face of Christ, light of heaven,
Face of Christ, most glorious,
Face of Christ, most lovable,
Face of Christ, most amiable,
Face of Christ, most fair,
Face of Christ, most precious,
Face of Christ, full of beauty in Your crib at Bethlehem,
Face of Christ, fondly caressed and tenderly kissed by Your Mother Mary,
Face of Christ, handsome as a youth in Nazareth,
Face of Christ, worn with exhaustion, labor and suffering, as You went about preaching the Good News to all men,

Have mercy on me.

Face of Christ, most desolate in the Garden of
    Gethsemane,*
Face of Christ, given the "kiss of death" by
    Judas,
Face of Christ, brutally gashed by the scourg-
    ing at the pillar,
Face of Christ, full of blood, blood which flowed
    freely from Your sacred head, as You were
    cruelly crowned with knife-like thorns,
Face of Christ, unjustly slapped by a servant
    of the high priest,
Face of Christ, unmercifully struck blows by the
    soldiers' powerful fists,
Face of Christ, spat upon,
Face of Christ, full of tears, sweat, dirt and
    blood, as You bravely carried Your cross to
    Calvary,
Face of Christ, kicked most viciously as You
    pathetically fell to the ground,
Face of Christ, imprinted on Veronica's veil,
Face of Christ, full of pain and anguish, pity and
    mercy, as You were dying upon the bitter
    wood of the holy cross,
Face of Christ, mirror of divine love,
Face of Christ, mirror of divine mercy,
Face of Christ, mirror of peace,
Face of Christ, mirror of resignation,
Face of Christ, mirror of meekness and of pa-
    tience,

*Have mercy on me.

Face of Christ, mirror of spiritual strength,*
Face of Christ, the staff of the weak,
Face of Christ, divine comforter of all who suffer physically, mentally, emotionally or spiritually,
Face of Christ, You are the sure salvation of all who look upon You with pity, compassion and love,
Face of Christ, when I am sad, depressed and lonely, console me.
Face of Christ, when I am about to lose all hope, and to despair, save me.
Face of Christ, when I am in darkness, illuminate my path.
Face of Christ, when I am restless, disturbed, have pity on me, and soothe me.
Face of Christ, may Your indescribable beauty be the great delight and pure joy of my soul for all eternity.

Have mercy on me.

A Prayer to Mary

Dear Blessed Mother Mary,
see how much I suffer in this vale of tears.
Take pity on me, please,
and intercede with Jesus
that He may make me well again.

However, if it is His holy will
that I continue to carry this particular cross
of sickness and distress,
then pray, dear Mother,
that I may suffer well;
in a Christian manner;
in a manner pleasing to your divine Son.

Pray that I may endure all things with faith—
believing that God wouldn't send me any cross
unless I could bear it,
and it was for the good of my soul
and the souls of others.

Pray that I may endure all things with hope—
trusting myself completely in Jesus' sacred
    hands.

Pray that I may endure all things with love—
loving Him who suffered so much for me,
and who loves me with an eternal love.

Pray that I may endure all things with patience
    and resignation,
following Your Son's fine example
in the Garden of Olives and on Mount Calvary.

And finally help me to suffer with good cheer—
even though it may hurt the more to smile.

All, all—just for dear Jesus,
and for you, my own dear Mother!

PRAYERS FOR SUNDAY

Jesus, who suffered a bloody sweat
in Your agony in the Garden of Olives,
have mercy on me.

Jesus, who felt abandoned by God
during Your agony in the Garden of Olives,
have mercy on me.

Jesus, who in the Garden
was the most abandoned of all the abandoned,
have mercy on me.

Lord, why do You stand off and hide Yourself
in times of distress?

When I call, answer me, O God,
from anguish rescue me,
have mercy on me and hear me.

To my words give ear, O Lord,
and heed my groaning.

Lord, heal me,
my body and soul are racked with pain.

Save me in Your merciful love.

I am exhausted with my groaning;
every night I drench my pillow with tears;
my eyes waste away with grief,
have mercy on me.

How long, O Lord, will You forget me?
How long will You hide Your face?
How long must I bear grief in my soul;
this sorrow in my heart day and night?
How long shall my enemies prevail?

Do not leave me alone in my distress,
come close, there is none else to help.

O Lord, do not leave me alone, my strength,
make haste to help me.

Relieve the anguish of my heart
and set me free from all distress.
See my affliction
and take all my sins away.

Preserve my life and rescue me.
Do not disappoint me;
You are my refuge.

Do not abandon or forsake me,
O God, my help.

Teach me to do Your will, O Lord,
for You are my God.

Jesus, sanctify our sufferings and sorrows.

Jesus, light of those in mental depression
or spiritual desolation,
have mercy on me.

Jesus, our refuge, have mercy on me.

Jesus, true light, have mercy on me.

Sacred Heart of Jesus, full of sadness,
have mercy on me.

Sacred Heart of Jesus, most desolate,
have mercy on me.

Agonizing Heart of Jesus,
be my consolation in my hours of depression.

Precious Blood of Jesus,
relief of the burdened, save me.

Precious Blood of Jesus,
stream of mercy, save me.

Precious Blood of Jesus,
be my refreshment.

Sacred Face of Jesus, full of anguish,
have mercy on me.

Sacred Face of Jesus, full of pity and mercy,
have mercy on me.

Passion of Christ, strengthen me.

Holy Spirit, Spirit of hope,
have mercy on me.

Holy Spirit, Spirit of fortitude,
have mercy on me.

Come, Holy Spirit,
and replace the tension within me
with a holy relaxation.

Mary, health of the sick,
heal my soul, my mind, my body.

Heart of Mary, be our model in suffering
and in tears;
be our support and consolation.

Mary, hope of the hopeless, pray for me.

O Mary, my hope, pray for me.

Mother of mercy, pray for me.

Loneliness of Mary, sustain me.

Mary, refuge of all sinners, pray for me.

Mary, hope of the hopeless, pray for me.

Through your powerful intercession,
dear Mother Mary,
may my heart be filled with holy hope,
so that in my darkest hours,
I may ever trust in God.

Virgin Mother, comfort my soul
troubled and afflicted in the midst of
many dangers that threaten me,
and the countless miseries that surround me.

Mary Immaculate, Mother of Consolation,
with all confidence I take refuge
in your most loving heart.

Mary, I beg of you,
listen graciously to the prayers
of this your poor servant,
a miserable sinner.

Mother of mercy, pity me.

Our Lady of divine compassion, pray for me.

Dear Mother, with firm confidence
I present myself before you,
for you are my most loving protectress.

With firm confidence, I come before you,
my most loving Mother,
afflicted and troubled as I am.

Mother, do not abandon your child,
for whom you have done so much already.

Mary, you are the sure hope of my salvation,
second only to your Son Jesus.

Preserve me, your child, O Mary,
from all evil;
let me enjoy the shelter of your peace and love.

PRAYERS FOR MONDAY

Jesus, who in the Garden
understood all mental suffering,
have mercy on me.

Jesus, who in the Garden
offered a haven to all who are forsaken,
have mercy on me.

From doubt about God's love
during my own nights in
"my Garden of Olives,"
deliver me, O Jesus.

Blessed be God, for while He scourges,
He has pity—He has pity
even while He punishes me for my sins.

O Lord, You are my shepherd,
I want for nothing—even though I walk
in a dark valley;
I will fear no evil for You are with me.

Keep me, O Lord, as the apple of Your eye.

Protect me, O Lord,
under the shadow of Your wings.

Jesus, consolation of the lonely,
have mercy on me.

Jesus, strength of the sick,
have mercy on me.

Jesus, be my friend and companion in suffering.

Sacred Heart of Jesus, our true peace,
have mercy on me.

Precious Blood of Jesus,
victor over demons, save me.

Precious Blood of Jesus,
courage of martyrs, save me.

Precious Blood of Jesus, be my consolation.

Passion of Christ, comfort me.

Sacred Face of Christ, most desolate,
have mercy on me.

Holy Spirit, Spirit of patience,
have mercy on me.

Holy Spirit, Spirit of long-suffering,
have mercy on me.

Holy Spirit,
replace the turbulence within me
with a sacred calm.

Holy Mary, full of compassion for those in need,
pray for me.

Our Lady of Hope, pray for me.

Our Lady of Consolation,
pray for me.

Our Lady of Pity,
pray for me.

Our Lady of good health,
pray for me.

Be gracious to me, your child,
dear Mother Mary,
and do not allow me to be overcome in my
    temptations.

With your loving consolation
relieve my troubled soul, dear Mother.

Watch over me, Mother,
and protect me from all evil.

Show me your tender mercy, Mother,
and I shall be refreshed
on this earthly pilgrimage of life.

Have pity on me, Mary, Mother of my soul,
and grant me consolation in my trials.

Present my cause to the Lord,
and spare me all further distress.

Deliver me from my fears, Mother,
and sweeten all my bitter pain.

Shed upon me the rays of your kindness
and enlighten me with the splendors
of your tender compassion.

Mary, do not abandon me, a miserable sinner.

Holy Mother, help of the helpless,
pray for me.

Mary, strength of the fearful,
pray for me.

Mary, comfort of the sorrowful,
pray for me.

Have pity on me, Mother,
and show me your tender mercy;
for you are the hope
and light of all who trust in you.

O Mary, grant me health of mind, body
and soul.

Mother of grace and life,
of mercy and hope,
turn to me your most kind face.
Raise me up to the state of perfect
friendship with God.
And obtain for me the grace of final per-
severance.

My Mother, remember the tears
which you freely shed on Calvary,
and have pity on me now.

PRAYERS FOR TUESDAY

From bitterness over "my own bitter
agony in the Garden,"
deliver me, O Jesus.

From despair in my moments of abandonment,
deliver me, O Jesus.

Teach me Your surrender to the will of the
      Father
in the Garden,
I pray You, hear me, O Lord.

Have mercy on me, O Lord, in Your kindness.

Do not, O Lord, cast me away from Your
      presence,
nor deprive me of Your Holy Spirit.

Spent and utterly crushed,
I cry aloud in anguish of heart.

O God, help me,
I am bowed down and brought to my knees.
I go mourning all the day long.

O Lord, do not forsake me.
My God, do not stay afar off.

Help me, O God; in You rests all my hope.

Take away Your scourge from me.
I am crushed by the blows of Your hand.

O Lord, turn Your ear to my cry.
Do not be deaf to my tears.

For Your name's sake, O Lord, save my life;
save my soul from distress.

My life is crushed to the ground.
I walk in darkness—
like the dead long forgotten;
help me! Give me light!

In the morning let me know Your love:
for I put my trust in You.

Make me know the way I should walk:
for to You I lift up my soul.

To You, O Lord, I call;
my Rock, hear me.
If You do not heed,
I shall become like those in the grave.

Have mercy on me, O Lord:
for I am in distress.
Tears have wasted my eyes,
my throat and my heart.

Jesus, light of the world,
enlighten the darkness of my mind.

Jesus, be my friend and companion in my
loneliness.

Jesus, teach me to be patient and resigned
to the will of God.

Jesus, strengthen me in times
of nervous depression and spiritual desolation.

All for You, O Sacred Heart of Jesus,
through the Immaculate Heart of Mary.

Sacred Heart of Jesus, author of all consolation,
have mercy on me.

Sacred Heart of Jesus, most patient,
have mercy on me.

Precious blood of Jesus, solace in sorrow,
save me.

Sacred Face of Christ,
hope of those about to despair,
have mercy on me.

Through Your agony and passion, Jesus,
deliver me from evil.

Holy Spirit, replace the anxiety within me
with a quiet confidence.

Holy Spirit, replace the fear within me
with a strong faith.

Holy Spirit, replace the bitterness within me,
with the sweetness of Your grace.

Mary, in every trial, every temptation,
every need, every danger, pray for me.

Sorrows of Mary, console me.

Mary, you cure the sick, cure me.

Mary, comfort me in my sorrow.

Mary, solace to those in trouble and affliction,
pray for me.

Mary, I am fearful, give me confidence.

Mary, I am restless, give me peace.

With you, sorrowful Mother,
I will gladly suffer all the trials,
misunderstandings and pains which it shall
please the Lord to send me.

Mary, refuge and hope of sinners,
pray for me.

Mother, hold out your hand to this fallen
wretch.

Mother, I know that with your help
I will conquer.

Mother, come to my aid,
for I commend myself to you.

Be gracious to me
and do not allow me to be overcome in my
temptations.

Have pity on me, O Mother Mary,
and keep my soul from all danger.

Obtain for my heart true courage
and holy patience
to bear the sufferings and trials of this difficult
life.

Console me, O Mother, in my day of suffering.

Mother, enlighten me with your wisdom.

Mother, show me your mercy.

Mother, turn my sadness into joy.
Fill my heart with the sweetness of your love,
and make me forget the miseries of this life.

O Mary, shed upon me the rays of your
kindness.

PRAYERS FOR WEDNESDAY

Give me the disposition of Your heart
during those hours in the Garden of Olives,
I pray You, hear me, O Jesus.

Give me strength and patience
in my trials and abandonment,
I pray You, hear me, O Jesus.

Send me Your consoling angel
at the time of my suffering,
in "my own Garden of Olives."

Distress and anguish have come upon me—
still let Your commandments be my delight.

Have pity on me, O Lord,
behold the afflictions I suffer.

O Lord, my God,
I cry to You: heal me.

Hear my voice, O God, when I complain:
preserve my life from the terror of the foe.

Behold my misery and my pain,
and forgive me all my sins.

Look upon my misery and rescue me.

O Lord, when my strength fails
forget me not.

Forsake not the works of Your hands.

I am wretched and in pain,
may Your help, O Lord, protect me.

Remember how frail You have made all men.

O Lord, give Your strength to Your servant.

Out of the depths I cry to you, O Lord;
Lord, hear my voice!
O let Your ears be attentive to the voice
of my pleading.

Sweet Jesus, I offer You,
through the Immaculate Heart of Mary,
the treasure of all my physical and mental suffer-
    ings.

Jesus, strengthen me in my periods of mental
    depression
and spiritual desolation.

Jesus, help me in time of loneliness.

Jesus, strengthen me when I am tempted
to lose all hope and to despair.

Sacred Heart of Jesus, most merciful,
have mercy on me.

Sacred Heart of Jesus, most abandoned,
have mercy on me.

All for You, dear Sacred Heart of Jesus,
through the Sorrowful Heart of Mary.

Precious Blood of Jesus, hope of the sick,
save me.

Precious Blood of Jesus, be my strength.

My Jesus Crucified,
have pity on me and on all
who suffer emotionally.

Sacred Face of Christ, solace of the sick,
have mercy on me.

Sacred Face of Christ, consolation of the
    suffering,
and of the sorrowing,
have mercy on me.

Sacred Face of Christ, mirror of resignation,
have mercy on me.

Holy Spirit of mercy, have mercy on me.

Holy Spirit, Spirit of sweetness, have mercy
    on me.

Holy Spirit, Spirit of consolation, have mercy
    on me.

Holy Spirit, be my comforter.

Holy Spirit, replace the darkness within me
with a gentle, soft light.

Heart of Mary, most compassionate,
be my consolation in the sorrows
and suffering of this life.

Mother, most sorrowful, pray for me.

Mother, most tearful, pray for me.

Mother, most afflicted, pray for me.

Mother, into your hands I entrust my soul,
mind and body; my whole life.

Mary, comfort me when I am in pain
of mind, body and soul.

Mother, soothe me with your sweetness.

Have pity on me, Mother,
and heal the wounds of my soul.

Mother, remove the sorrows and worries
of my soul.

Have pity on me, O Mary, and show me your
mercy;
for you are the hope and the light of all who
trust in you.

O Mother, your mercy and kindness
are proclaimed everywhere:
God has blessed the works of your hands.

Mary, console the brokenhearted,
and refresh me with your motherly love.

Behold my misery, glorious Virgin,
and delay not to aid me in time of trouble.

My Mother, do not abandon me in my distress.

Mary, support me with your refreshing help.

In dangers and doubts grant your aid, O Mary,
and in all trials may I find your gracious
presence.

Mother, because I hope in you,
I shall not lose my soul.

Watch over me, dear Mother,
and protect me from all evil;
be with me to the very end,
and I shall find eternal life.

PRAYERS FOR THURSDAY

Teach me to watch and to pray with You
always in the Garden,
I pray You, hear me, O Jesus.

Let me recognize my suffering
as a share in Your own suffering,
I pray You, hear me, O Jesus.

Teach me to pray when I feel weak and discouraged,
I pray You, hear me, O Jesus.

Hear my prayers, O Lord, listen to my cry;
be not indifferent to my tears.

Relieve the anguish of my heart, O Lord,
and free me from all worries.

How long will You hide Your face from me?
How long shall I harbor sorrow in my soul?
Look on me—answer me, O Lord, my God.

O Lord, turn Your ear to my cry.
Do not be deaf to my tears.

When I call, answer me, O Lord;
from anguish release me;
have mercy, and hear me!

Save me in Your merciful love.

Do not leave me alone in my distress;
come close, there is none else to help me.

Redeem me, O God, from all my distress.

Passion of Christ, be my comfort.

Sacred Face of Christ, solace of all who suffer physically, mentally, emotionally or spiritually, have mercy on me.

Sacred Heart of Jesus, most desolate, have mercy on me.

Sacred Heart of Jesus, pierced with a lance, have mercy on me.

Heart of Jesus, salvation of all those who call on You,
have mercy on me.

Blood of Christ, be my refreshment.

Precious Blood of Jesus, hope of the sick, save me.

Precious Blood of Jesus, be my strength.

Holy Spirit, deliver me from despondency and despair.

Holy Spirit, the consoler, have mercy on me and console me.

Holy Spirit, replace the coldness within me with a loving warmth.

Mary, crucified in heart, pray for me.

Heart of Mary, be my consolation in all my trials.

Sorrowful Mother, most sad, pray for me.

Sorrowful Mother, fountain of tears, pray
for me.

In You, Mother, I place all my hope,
because of your loving compassion.

O Mary, bring me safe through every danger.

O Mary, in the storms of affliction give me your
sure and powerful protection.

Dear Mother, turn your motherly gaze upon me.

O Mary, from you I hope for peace in sorrows;
light in my doubts; protection in my dangers;
help in all my needs.

O Mary, the consoler, be my refuge, my
strength,
my consolation.

O Mary, be my hope, my refuge, my protection,
my guide.

O my Mother, comfort me in the midst of all my
trials.

Take up my cause, Mother of mine,
for I have sadly departed from my innocence;
but because I hope in you,
I shall not lose my soul.

Into your loving and tender hands, Mother,
I entrust my soul, my whole life
and the hour of my death.

PRAYERS FOR FRIDAY

When You share with me Your hours of agony
in the Garden of Olives, have mercy on me.

When sorrow and sadness, disgust and anguish
overshadow me as they did You,
have mercy on me.

When the light of Faith seems to be going out
during my night of suffering,
have mercy on me.

O God, listen to my prayer,
do not hide from my pleading,
attend to me and reply;
with my cares, I cannot rest.

My heart is stricken within me,
death's terror is on me,
trembling and fear fall upon me,
and horror overwhelms me.

I am wearied with my crying,
and my throat is parched.
My eyes are wasted away from looking for my
    God.

Lord, answer me, for Your love is kind;
in Your compassion, turn to me.

Lord, my God, I call for help by day;
I cry at night before You.
Let my prayer come into Your presence.

O Lord, turn Your ear to my cry!

O come and deliver Your friend!

Give me help, O God, against the foe.

Rescue me, O Lord, from my many enemies:
I have fled to You for refuge.

Dear Jesus, take pity on me,
and help me and all those tempted against the
virtue of hope.

Dear Jesus, help me and all the lonely and
depressed.

Jesus, let Your peace reign in my heart.

Jesus, help all of us who are emotionally sick.
Give us strength, patience, comfort, hope,
health—
the grace to do Your blessed will.

Sacred Heart of Jesus, in hours of loneliness
and abandonment, give me the companionship
and the shelter of Your most agonizing Heart.

Remember, O Jesus, Your creature whom
You have redeemed by Your Precious Blood.

My Jesus Crucified, whose most pure soul
was sorrowful unto death, have mercy on me.

O scourges of Christ, deliver me from despair!

Jesus Crucified, I trust in You; I hope in You;
I love You.

Sacred Face of Christ, full of pity and mercy,
have mercy on me.

Sacred Face of Christ, most desolate,
have mercy on me.

Spirit of hope, have mercy on me.

Holy Spirit, Spirit of joy and peace,
have mercy on me.

Holy Spirit, replace the night within me
with Your day.

From the snares of the evil spirit,
deliver me, O Holy Spirit.

Hail, Holy Queen, Mother of mercy;
hail, my life, my sweetness and my hope.

O Mary, let me be full of hope and confidence.

Heart of Mary, my hope, pray for me.

Mother of Sorrows, give peace to my heart.

In all my tribulations
of soul, mind and body,
help me, O Sorrowful Mother.

O Mary, my only hope after Jesus, take pity
on me.

O Mary, you are my refuge in my urgent need.

Have pity on me, Mother,
and show me your mercy,
for you are the hope and the light of all who
trust in you.

Mary, hope of the desperate, pray for me.

Mary, hope of the abandoned, pray for me.

Holy Mother, strengthen me against despair
at the sight of my sins
which the devil brings before me.

Holy Mother, I put all my hope in you.

The burden of my sins oppresses me, dear Lady,
and my weakness discourages me.
I am beset by fear and temptation, have pity
on me
and plead to the Lord for me.

O Mother of mercy, have pity on me in my
distress.

Mary, by your grace deliver me from the hands
of the evil one who is threatening me.

Show me your mercy, dear Lady, and pray
for me;
turn my sadness into true joy.

PRAYERS FOR SATURDAY

When hope seems to be giving way to despair
during "my hours in the garden,"
have mercy on me, Lord.

When God's love seems to have died in me
during "my hours in the garden,"
have mercy on me, Lord.

When I am tempted to exaggerate my suffering
and pity myself,
Lord, have mercy on me.

When the Father does not seem to hear my
prayers,
Lord, have mercy on me.

O Lord, remember me out of the love
You have for Your people.

Help me, Lord God;
save me because of Your love for me.

Let Your face shine on Your servant;
save me in Your love.

O Lord, how long will You look on?
Come to my rescue!

Spent and utterly crushed,
I cry aloud in anguish of heart.

Do not cast me away from Your presence,
nor deprive me of Your Holy Spirit.

Come to my help, O Lord, lest I perish.

O Lord, do not forsake me!
Our God, do not stay afar off!
Make haste and come to my help,
my Lord, my God and Savior.

Save me in Your merciful love!

Lord, heal me; my soul is racked with pain.

Turn to me and have mercy:
for I am poor and lonely.

Redeem me and show me Your mercy!

Have mercy on me, O Lord,
for I am in distress.

My God, my God, why have You forsaken me!

O Lord, help me—my one companion in darkness.

O Lord, the bread I eat is ashes;
my drink is mingled with tears.

O Lord, help me,
for my tears have become my bread,
by night and by day.

Give me joy to balance my affliction!

Jesus, flood my soul with Your grace;
flood my mind with Your light;
flood my heart with Your peace.

Jesus, in time of weakness be my fortitude.

Jesus, in periods of doubts, be my safe guide.

Jesus, in time of desolation, come to me,
and be my sole consolation.

Jesus, in time of darkness of spirit,
come and be my sure light.

Jesus, I hope in You.

O Sacred Heart of Jesus,
I believe in Your love for me.

Sacred Heart of Jesus, I hope in You;
I place my full confidence in You.

Sacred Heart of Jesus, strengthened in Your
agony
by an angel, comfort me in my present agony of
mind and soul.

Blood of Christ, be my support.

Blood of Christ, be my consolation.

Blood of Christ, stream of mercy, save me.

My Jesus Crucified, I put my trust in You.

My Jesus Crucified, I hope in You.

Passion of Christ, be my strength.

Sacred Face of Christ, hope of the despairing,
have mercy on me.

Sacred Face of Christ, solace of the sick,
and of all those who suffer, have mercy on me.

From despondency and despair, deliver me,
O Holy Spirit.

Holy Spirit, You are the Dove
that gives peace to weary souls;
give me peace and rest.

Holy Spirit, the Divine Consoler, have mercy
on me.

Holy Spirit, replace the winter within me
with Your everlasting spring.

Our Lady of Mental Peace, pray for me.

Heart of Mary, seat of mercy, pray for me.

Heart of Mary, full of compassion for those in
need, pray for me.

Mother, who stood by Jesus in His agony, pray
for me.

Mary, put a trusting smile on my face.

Mary, I am fearful, give me confidence.

Mother, you are my light in uncertainty,
my comfort in sorrow,
my consolation in trial, my refuge from every
danger.

Mary, I am afflicted with many sorrows
in my body and soul, and I take refuge, like a
child,
in the embrace of your motherly protection.

O Mary, make me strong in the midst of the
temptations
and bitterness which so often trouble my soul.

Mother, I am afflicted with miseries
both spiritual and temporal—
have pity on me and pray to Jesus for me.

Mother of Good Hope, pray for me.

Graciously hear me, O Mary,
a miserable sinner who trusts your tender
    mercy.

Come to my aid, O Mary, in all my trials.

O Mary, deliver me from all evils and dangers
which threaten my body, mind and soul.

Fill my heart with your sweetness, most loving
    Virgin,
and make me forget the miseries of this life.

Have pity on me, Queen of glory and honor
and keep my soul from all danger.

APPENDIX

SAINT THERESE
SAINT OF THE EMOTIONALLY ILL

St. Therese was called a "subject of compulsion neurosis." She was stricken by scrupulosity. She suffered periods of depression.

At the tender age of ten, the Little Flower was overcome by a terrible and mysterious illness. Was it a serious nervous breakdown that she suffered? Today some experts say yes. For instance, John Beevers says this in his book, *St. Therese, the Making of a Saint:* "No name was given to her complaint, but it was *obviously* what we in non-technical terms would call a *nervous breakdown.*"

No doctor, no medicine and no treatment could be of any help to the pitiful child. However, she was finally aided. Her help came from heaven. Mary herself, the Mother of God, intervened, and Therese was cured, cured in a twinkling of an eye!

Yes, little Therese was cured. Yes, she was out of danger. She didn't die as a result of the strange sickness; nor did she go insane as it was at first feared.

In spite of the cure, St. Therese remained a very nervous and a very sensitive person. In curing her, God did not destroy her emotions; nor did He change her melancholic temperament; nor her psychic personality.

No, not all of the Little Flower's emotional troubles were over after the Blessed Mother smiled on her and cured her.

St. Therese still had some nervous symptoms. (A nun's rattling rosary almost sent St. Therese into a nervous spell.) She was to remain scrupulous for many years. She still had some neurotic tendencies—but, (and this is very important to remember!) in spite of all this, the Little Flower was always cheerful and most patient. She was full of humility and courage. She was totally resigned to the will of God. She was ever serene, ever full of confidence in God.

Our age is the age of mental suffering. And St. Therese can rightly be called the saint of our age. She, more than any other saint, ought to be venerated as the patroness of all those who suffer from emotional and mental disorders.

Let those who have any emotional or mental problems take heart. Let them use St. Therese for their example; for example par excellence she is. Let them take her as their friend and patroness—for, if they do, one day they too will be numbered among the saints, in spite (*and maybe because of*) their deformed psychic structures. Let neurotics and the scrupulous look at the life of the Little Flower, and say: "This is the 'stuff' saints are made of. We can hope for sanctity. We can become saints. We *must* become saints. And this is the meaning for our mental suffering."

PRAYERS TO ST. THERESE

Dear St. Therese,
wonderful Little Flower of God,
you know and understand emotional illness
because you, too, were greatly troubled
in this manner.
However, dear Saint,
you were miraculously cured
by the Blessed Mother herself.

O good and most dear Saint,
pray to our heavenly Mother for me,
that through her wonderful and powerful
intercession,
I may soon obtain the health of mind
and peace of soul that I long for,
and for which I hope and pray.

St. Therese,
consoler of troubled souls,
and special friend and advocate
of all those who suffer from nervous
and mental disorders,
please pray for me,
and for all who are emotionally
or mentally afflicted.
Amen.

St. Therese, you were once cured of an emotional illness, pray that I may now be cured of mine.

St. Therese, comfort of the despondent, pray for me.

St. Therese, consoler of the afflicted, pray for me.

St. Therese, special friend of those who suffer from nervous and mental disorders, pray for me.

St. Therese, light of those in darkness, pray for me.

St. Therese, lover of crosses, pray for me.

St. Therese, most patient in suffering, pray for me.

St. Therese, healer of the sick, pray for me.

St. Therese, remarkable for trust in God, pray for me.

St. Therese, lover of patience, pray for me.

St. Therese, mirror of resignation, pray for me.

St. Therese, curing my bodily and emotional ills, pray for me.

St. Therese, comforter of troubled hearts, pray for me.

St. Therese, powerful advocate with God, pray for me.

St. Therese, helper in all adversities, pray for me.

St. Therese, defend me in conflict, and pray for me.

St. Therese, hope of mental sufferers, pray for me.

St. Therese, consolation of the suffering, pray for me.

St. Therese, hope of the sick, pray for me.

St. Paul Book & Media Centers

ALASKA
750 West 5th Ave., Anchorage, AK
  99501; 907-272-8183

CALIFORNIA
3908 Sepulveda Blvd., Culver City, CA
  90230; 310-397-8676
5945 Balboa Ave., San Diego, CA
  92111; 619-565-9181
46 Geary Street, San Francisco, CA
  94108; 415-781-5180

FLORIDA
145 S.W. 107th Ave., Miami, FL
  33174; 305-559-6715

HAWAII
1143 Bishop Street, Honolulu, HI
  96813; 808-521-2731

ILLINOIS
172 North Michigan Ave., Chicago, IL
  60601; 312-346-4228

LOUISIANA
4403 Veterans Memorial Blvd.,
  Metairie, LA 70006; 504-887-7631

MASSACHUSETTS
50 St. Paul's Ave., Jamaica Plain,
  Boston, MA 02130; 617-522-8911
Rte. 1, 885 Providence Hwy.,
  Dedham, MA 02026; 617-326-5385

MISSOURI
9804 Watson Rd., St. Louis, MO
  63126; 314-965-3512

NEW JERSEY
561 U.S. Route 1, Wick Plaza,
  Edison, NJ 08817; 908-572-1200

NEW YORK
150 East 52nd Street, New York, NY
  10022; 212-754-1110
78 Fort Place, Staten Island, NY
  10301; 718-447-5071

OHIO
2105 Ontario Street (at Prospect
  Ave.), Cleveland, OH 44115;
  216-621-9427

PENNSYLVANIA
Northeast Shopping Center, 9171-A
  Roosevelt Blvd. (between Grant Ave.
  & Welsh Rd.), Philadelphia, PA
  19114; 610-277-7728

SOUTH CAROLINA
243 King Street, Charleston, SC
  29401; 803-577-0175

TENNESSEE
4811 Poplar Ave., Memphis, TN
  38117 901-761-2987

TEXAS
114 Main Plaza, San Antonio, TX
  78205; 210-224-8101

VIRGINIA
1025 King Street, Alexandria, VA
  22314; 703-549-3806

GUAM
285 Farenholt Avenue, Suite 308,
  Tamuning, Guam 96911;
  671-649-4377

CANADA
3022 Dufferin Street, Toronto, Ontario,
  Canada M6B 3⁻5; 416-781-9131